KT-225-094

Foreword

by Joyce McMillan

FOR THOUSANDS OF YEARS we human beings have had the luxury of defining ourselves in opposition to other groups of people. If we wanted to know exactly who we were—to feel "at home" either geographically or psychologically—all we had to do was to say who we were not; us not them, Scottish not English, British not German, Christian not heathen, Protestant not Catholic, or vice versa. Sometimes we even tended to talk as if "we", on our side of the divide, represented humanity and those others, on the opposite side, were somehow less human, little more than animals. In the heat of conflict we can still hear that language being used across the world today. But if we look with clear eyes at the world of the 21st century we can see that these divisive ways of identifying and defining ourselves are crumbling. The pace and intensity of global travel and communications, and the reality of rapid migration and multicultural living in many modern communities, means we can no longer, or only with increasing effort and denial, sustain the myth that "they" are somehow categorically different from "us". Now we can see, from day to day, how human beings everywhere wrestle with the same fears, the same yearnings, the same search for spiritual comfort and meaning, and the same hopes for their children.

So how do we define our sense of belonging now? This study guide suggests some ways of thinking about this key question of our time, within a framework of Christian belief and prayer. It also recalls one of the most radical aspects of the faith: its vision of a kingdom in which distinctions of class, gender and tribe will wither away, and in which our sense of identity will become both more individual in its appreciation of each precious life, and more universal in its sense of deep connection with the whole human family.

Joyce McMillan

Introduction

Where the heart is...

"Lore looks forward to the silence at Oma's, to Wiebke's smiles, and Liesel's cake. She looks forward to when there will be no more ruins, only new houses, and she won't remember any more how it was before."

from Rachel Seiffert's novel, *The Dark Room*

Lore is a twelve-year-old girl who leads her younger sister and brothers across Germany in the weeks after the end of the war in 1945. Their parents have been captured and imprisoned so they head for their Grandmother's house in Hamburg. Amidst the ruins, they will begin the process of rebuilding lives and trying to understand what has led them to this point. The story is a story of migration, of home, of loss and of lies. It deals with memory and survival and with the sheer courage and persistence of a girl looking for home.

Our continent is profoundly shaped by the effects of the major European wars of the last century. The homes we have made, the borders that enclose us, the way we do politics and the books we read all bear the marks of those conflicts. In our own day, the same realities continue to be shaped by the big picture. Conflicts in the Gulf, the global flow of capital and goods and the plight of peoples without a homeland make an impact in communities of every sort.

At the same time, we find ourselves celebrating a new awareness of our human diversity, wondering about the fluid nature of what we see as our identity and feeling anxiety about the security of our nations and neighbourhoods. At another level, we have welcomed both *The Big Issue* and *Changing Rooms* into our cultural landscape, aware of the tension expressed there.

Our Christian faith has much to say about our sense of home. We inherit the tradition of the Hebrew prophets who speak

Where the heart is.....

a five week study guide for ecumenical groups

"It is through faith that all of you are God's sons in union with Christ Jesus. You were baptized into union with Christ, and now you are clothed, so to speak, with the life of Christ himself. So there is no difference between Jews and Gentiles, between slaves and free men, between men and women; you are all one in union with Christ Jesus. If you belong to Christ, then you are the descendants of Abraham and will receive what God has promised."

Galatians 3: 26-29 (Good News)

Edited by Kate Fenn-Tye

ACTS

Action of Churches Together in Scotland

Published and produced by ACTS:
Action of Churches Together in Scotland (ACTS)
Scottish Churches House, Dunblane FK15 0AJ
Tel 01786 823588; Fax 01786 825844;
Email acts.ecum@dial.pipex.com
www.acts-scotland.org

Registered charity number: SC 013196
ISBN 0 86153 401 8

Copyright © Action of Churches Together in Scotland 2002

All rights reserved. Churches and church organisations have permission to reproduce this publication in part for local use, provided the copies include the above copyright notice and no charge is made for them. Any other reproduction, storage or transmission of material from this publication by any means or in any form, electronic or mechanical, including photocopying, recording, or any information storage and retrieval system requires written permission, which should be sought from the Administrator, Action of Churches Together in Scotland, Scottish Churches House, Dunblane FK15 0AJ, Tel: 01786 823588

Further copies available from ACTS.

Cover design by Wendy Ball, 2ND STOREY, Edinburgh.

The art work used in the cover design was produced by service users of *Move On* and was displayed in an exhibition at the Intermedia Gallery in Glasgow in July 2001.

Move On is a charity that provides a range of services in Glasgow and Edinburgh to people who have experienced homelessness.

For more information please phone 0141 221 2272 or 0131 524 9870.

Illustrations by Cat Outram

Design and layout by Kate Fenn-Tye

Formatted and printed by Lothian Print, 7 New Lairdship Yards
Edinburgh EH11 3UY

Contents

About the writing team

Alastair Cameron
Alastair Cameron was the first member of staff of the Scottish Churches Housing Agency in 1994. He has worked in homelessness in Scotland since the mid-1980s, following a time as a community worker in Lancashire. When not campaigning against homelessness, he raises his children, digs his allotment or plays traditional music. He is a member of the Religious Society of Friends (Quakers).

Kate Fenn-Tye
Kate Fenn-Tye used to work in communications in the corporate sector and then for the Scottish Episcopal Church. She now spends most of her time caring for three young children, as well as undertaking writing and editorial work on ecumenical projects. She is a member of Stirling Baptist Church.

Ed Hone CSsR
Ed Hone is a Redemptorist : a member of an international Roman Catholic Religious Order dedicated to Mission. Ed is based in St. Patrick's parish in the centre of Edinburgh where, with his Redemptorist community, he runs a Mission Development project.

Maggie Lunan
Maggie Lunan has been Education Adviser for Christian Aid Scotland for ten years. She has a dual remit; firstly for education in the church sector (clergy and lay) considering world issues in the light of gospel values, secondly for the formal sector, working with teachers and teachers in training, as well as in curriculum development. She is a member of the Church of Scotland.

Nikki Macdonald
Having grown up in Australia, Nikki moved to the UK in January 1992. She has worked for the Iona Community on the Isle of Iona and is currently an Associate of the Community. Having a Catholic mother, a Free Church of Scotland father, Nikki was christened into the Anglican Communion and spent ten years in the Uniting Church in Australia. She is now involved in the Scottish Episcopal Church, and currently works for Cornerstone Bookshop, Edinburgh, an ecumenical resource for the Church in Scotland.

Stephen Smyth
Stephen Smyth is a member of the Marist Brothers, a Roman Catholic Religious Order. He has worked in secondary schools and adult faith development. Currently he is Ecumenical Officer for Glasgow Churches Together and is a member of the Contextual Bible Study Group. He also writes poetry and liturgical material under his full name: Stephen Eric Smyth.

strongly against the abuse of the land and the annexation of the homes of the poor. The Hebrew Torah makes sure that the 'alien' has the protection of a home and a community. Even the perpetrator of a culpable homicide is offered a place of safety. On top of these affirmations of God's justice, the New Testament adds in the incarnation of God in Jesus; we see the action of a God who "makes his home among us that we might forever dwell in him" (from Liturgy of the Scottish Episcopal Church, 1982). Home making and homecoming have a place even in the nature of God the Trinity.

The writers of this series of studies have brought together this rich mixture of stories and have offered ways for you to add your own. They invite you to travel to where the heart is through prayer, sharing and study. They invite you to make a home for the Word of God in the small community that will gather to share in these studies and from that home to continue, strengthened, on your pilgrimage together. We hope that the pilgrimage of your faith will be enriched by meeting new fellow-pilgrims; those with whom you share the studies and those beyond the group whose lives will become more known to you as you share. Their experience of home may be very different from yours and it may be that the interaction of our different experiences will lead us all to a deeper understanding of what home is, of who we are, and of who God is.

John McLuckie
Convener of ACTS Commission
for Justice, Peace, Social and Moral Issues

Running the study sessions – preparing and facilitating

Making the most of Where the heart is...

It is hoped that the group sessions from *'Where the heart is...'* will provide a reflective, encouraging and prayerful experience for all who take part in them. To enable the sessions to run as effectively as possible, all participants are encouraged to share in their preparation and facilitation. It may be helpful to agree for different people to look after different aspects of each session – from chairs to prayers. It is highly recommended that the facilitation of the formal part of the session be shared by two people working closely together as a team.

Each session contains some short notes for facilitators. It is hoped that the following, more general, notes help to make the facilitators' task less daunting and thus enable the sessions to be more enjoyable and beneficial for everyone involved.

A special thank you goes to all those who prepare and facilitate any part of the sessions for their generous service to their group.

About being facilitators

(1) General tips

The facilitators are the main enablers in the group. Their role is to help the session to run smoothly and to allow the experience to be as positive as possible. The facilitators have the main responsibility for creating the atmosphere for the session. This will include setting up a comfortable and welcoming space and establishing a sense of trust, mutual respect and sharing among the participants. The facilitators also have to try to keep the session to its agreed topic and time.

They should try to encourage aspects such as respect, dialogue, listening, exploration and the sharing of experience, understanding, belief, insight and story. They should try to avoid aspects such as debate, argument, intellectualisation, wandering off the topic or letting any one person dominate the group (including the facilitators themselves!).

Facilitators have to put more effort into asking key questions and listening to people's responses rather than talking themselves. Think in terms of inviting, but not forcing, others to share a response. Good questions are 'open' questions, like, 'Who? Why? What? How?...do you think/feel?' These allow people to tap into and share their own experience and understanding.

One useful technique for encouraging each person to share something is to break into groups of three (two or four can also work). Ask the threes to buzz for a few minutes on the question and then invite a little feedback from each of the small groups to the full group. This should be more like a 'flavour', rather than a 'summary', of what has been said. Particular points may then be explored further as a full group. (Breaking into threes can also be helpful if any one person is tending to dominate the full group.) Following a rhythm of reflecting alone, sharing in threes and exploring in the full group will often help the session reach deeper and more satisfying places. Working with another facilitator makes it much easier to manage all this. Agree between you who will be responsible for which question or part of the session.

(2) Before the session

Be as familiar as possible with the venue. Check the 'ordinary' things that are so important: that the room is comfortable and welcoming; that there are enough chairs; that the biscuits are ready.

Be as familiar as possible with the session, the topic and the material. If required, prepare photocopies or check that the CD is at the right track.

Many people create a centrepiece to help establish a visual focus which can help support this kind of reflection. The centrepiece may contain items such as a Bible, candle, coloured cloth, flowers or icon. Try to keep it simple and tasteful. You may choose to set this up before the formal session or at the start of it.

Some of these tasks may be taken on by other members of the group.

(3) At the start of the session

It helps at the start of a series of meetings to let everyone introduce themselves and to repeat this at later sessions if someone new comes along. Then take a few minutes to check in with how people are today, at the start of this particular session. Make sure that everyone knows how long the session is likely to last

Make a clear start to the formal part of the session. Remind everyone of the invitation to share and to share only what is comfortable and appropriate in this group. Avoid giving too long an introduction.

(4) During the session

As facilitators, have an idea of when you expect people to be reflecting quietly on their own, working in threes or working in the full group.

Keep looking around the group, being sensitive to people's body language. Encourage and invite them to contribute. You can make this invitation by word, look or gesture. If appropriate, you might seek some clarification of what someone has contributed. Not everyone is comfortable speaking out loud in a group. But, no matter how silent someone may appear, they will be reflecting on what is going on.

If reading aloud is required, remember that not everyone is comfortable doing so. At the start of the reading, when you are inviting people to read, say something like, 'if anyone is not comfortable reading out loud, just tap the person beside you and they will read on next.' This will help put everyone at their ease.

(5) After the session

Take a few moments to find out how people felt about the session. Confirm details for the next meeting and who will be taking responsibility for different parts of the preparation. Thank everyone for their participation.

And finally....Be creative in your facilitating. You bring plenty of your own skills and experience. Use them. Relax and enjoy this valuable service.

About the material

Timing. Each session offers material designed to last about 90 minutes, and suggested timings have been given for each section. If you want your study session to last longer, there is the opportunity to spend more time on certain parts of the session. In some cases additional ideas for discussion questions or reflection are included in the Notes for Facilitators which follow each session.

Worship. Each session includes suggestions for opening and closing worship, usually prayers, but you can of course devise your own worship material and encourage open prayer. In the Facilitators' Notes for each session you will find suggestions for hymns and worship songs. They can be found in:

- *Common Ground*—'a song book for all the churches', published by Saint Andrews Press
- *Songs of God's People*—published by Oxford University Press
- *Mission Praise*—published by Marshall Pickering

Reading out loud. There are many opportunities for group members to participate. Wherever possible ask different people to read scripture passages, poems, prayers. You may like to forewarn people, so that they have a chance to familiarise themselves with the material.

Welcome and looking back. Apart from session one, each session opens with a chance to recall the previous group meeting. The facilitator may like to give a brief recap on the previous study, inviting observations from the group on how they experienced the session. This will set the context for beginning the new study.

Moving forward in faith. This section appears towards the end of each session. It is an opportunity for summing up what people have experienced/learned, and for considering what they might take away with them for further thought, reflection, prayer or practical action. It is also a chance to look ahead and begin preparing for the next session.

Material for children

Material based on this study guide and suitable for use with children and young people can be found on the ACTS website:
www.acts-scotland.org

Session One: Where the heart is…

...*Belonging*

Welcome

[10 minutes]

Take a few minutes to welcome each other, and for people to introduce themselves to each other.

Introduction

[2 minutes]

Welcome to this first session of our exploration of 'Where the heart is'. Today we will be exploring together the theme of 'Belonging'.

Belonging is the feeling of being connected with other people or with a grouping of people or with a place or environment; the feeling of being a member and of having a proper place in some significant relationships. Belonging is a major factor in a person's sense of well-being.

Today we are invited to reflect on where and how we feel we belong in different contexts and to explore what this belonging means.

Secondly we are invited to share one passage of Scripture and try to discern what light Jesus' words may throw on our reflection about belonging.

Lastly we are challenged to consider how our being together as a group for this series of meetings will help us, individually and together, on the journey ahead, the journey of our lives and faith.

Opening Worship

You may wish to include music, and a group member may like to offer a prayer, or the following may be read by one or more people:

'A Prayer of Gathering'

All: **O Loving God,**
        you know who we are
        and where we are with our lives and consciences:

Solos: *– people who are content*
        and people who are discontent,
    – some who are certain
        and some who are uncertain,
    – Christians by conviction, Christians by convention
        and those who walk alongside in trust and solidarity,
    – those who believe, those who half-believe
        and those who disbelieve.

All: **God, our Creator,**
        you know where we have come from:

Solos: *– from our circle of family, friends and acquaintances*
        or from great loneliness,
    – from a life of quiet prosperity
        or from manifold confusion and distress,
    – from relationships that are well ordered
        or from those that are disordered or under stress
    – from a supportive and meaningful Christian community
        or from its outer edges,
    – from our variety of traditions
        and our variety of experiences.

All: **God, who sustains us all,**
        we gather before you now in all our differences

Solos: *– but alike in our human qualities and hopes*
        as well as in our frailties and mortality.

> – *Without your love and grace*
>   *we would be lost.*
> – *We gather here together in the name of your Son,*
>   *Jesus Christ, our hope and binding force.*
> – *We gather to praise you by our sharing*
>   *and by opening ourselves to hear you speaking to us in*
>   *our inner selves and through each other.*

All: *We ask that this may take place*
>   *here in our special time together*
> *and we ask this*
>   *in the name of Jesus, our Saviour and brother.*

Amen.

Karl Barth (adapted)

Exploring : the experience of 'belonging'   [25 minutes]

You are invited first to reflect and share some of your own personal experience of belonging and second to consider the wider human experience.

1. Identifying and reflecting on our own experience of belonging

Using the worksheet at the end of the session, think quietly about where you personally experience or don't experience a sense of belonging. Write a few significant examples on the graphic provided.

Think about why you have graded them as strong/moderate/ weak/ not at all. Share a little in threes and then in the full group.

2. Reflecting on our common human experience

Discuss the following questions, in view of what you have been sharing about your own personal experiences:

1. Generally, what kind of things help a person to feel that they belong in a place or relationship?

2. Generally, what kind of thing diminishes or destroys a person's sense of belonging?

Reading God's Word

We are now invited to allow the Scriptures to speak to us, and to consider what light they might bring to our understanding of belonging, particularly with regard to the Christian community.

Have the following passage read out loud once or twice:

John 10:1–16 (THE MESSAGE)

He calls his sheep by name

Let me set this before you as plainly as I can. If a person climbs over or through the fence of a sheep pen instead of going though the gate, you know he is up to no good – a sheep rustler! The shepherd walks right up to the gate. The gatekeeper opens the gate to him and the sheep recognise his voice. He calls his own sheep by name and leads them out. When he gets them all out, he leads them and they follow because they are familiar with his voice. They won't follow a stranger's voice but will scatter because they aren't used to the sound of it.

Jesus told this simple story, but they had no idea what he was talking about. So he tried again. "I'll be explicit, then. I am the Gate for the sheep. All those others are up to no good – sheep stealers, every one of them. But the sheep didn't listen to them. I am the Gate. Anyone who goes through me will be cared for – will freely go in and out, and find pasture. A thief is only there to steal and kill and destroy. I came so they can have real and eternal life, more and better life than they ever dreamed of.

"I am the Good Shepherd. The Good Shepherd puts the sheep before himself, sacrifices himself if necessary. A hired man is not a real shepherd. The sheep mean nothing to him. He sees a wolf come and runs for it, leaving the sheep to be ravaged and scattered by the wolf. He's only in it for the money. The sheep don't matter to him.

"I am the Good Shepherd. I know my own sheep and my own sheep know me. In the same way, the Father knows me and I know the Father. I put the sheep before myself, sacrificing myself if necessary. You need to know that I have other sheep in addition to those in this pen. I need to gather and bring them, too. They'll also recognise my voice. Then it will be one flock, one Shepherd."

Discussion   [25–35 minutes]

1. Look carefully at this text. What does it say to you about Jesus and about the relationship he is offering us?   [10–15 minutes]

2. Earlier, we explored the sense of 'belonging' at four levels: strong, moderate, weak, not at all.

How, do you think, would this passage speak to people who find themselves at each of the four different levels of belonging in terms of the Christian community?   [15–20 minutes]

(Note: There may be different interpretations of the phrase 'the Christian community' within your group. Respect these rather than seek an agreed 'definition'.)

Moving Forward in Faith   [10 minutes]

We have reflected together on our sense and experience of 'belonging'; we have shared our own experiences and explored the Scriptures. In the light of this experience, what practical difference might our reflection make to our journey of faith – as a group or as individuals – before we meet again?

Closing Worship and Thanks   [5–10 minutes]

During the closing worship a member of the group may wish to offer a prayer, and you may like to include worship songs.

One or more people may like to read the following prayer:

Special People

All: *We thank you, O God,*
           for those special people
           who are channels of your love in our lives:

Solo: *for those who gave us birth*
           and, in the weakness of our infancy,
           sheltered, nurtured and treasured us;

Solo: *for those who taught us to walk, to talk,*
          to explore tastes, smells and sounds
          and to experience the warmth of belonging and
          embracing;

Solo: *for those who overlooked our faults*
          and affirmed our strengths
          and for the friends, young and old,
          who share our tears and laughter.

Solo: *We thank you, Lord,*
          for the people of strong faith
          who stretch our minds and enlarge our capacity
          to explore and understand your ways;

Solo: *for those at every stage of our journey*
          who teach us trust by trusting us
          and who enable us to love others
          through the experience of being loved.

Solo: *We thank you, loving Creator,*
          for all those good and sincere people
          who have shown us the joys and disciplines
          that help us to build up your Kingdom

Solo: *and especially for the people who taught us to love you*
          rather than to be afraid of you.

All: *God of love, God of Jesus,*
          for these healing experiences of growth and loving
          and for the knowledge that the best is yet to come,
          we praise your holy name
          through Christ our Lord.

                                              Amen

Worksheet for 'Exploring' : Where I feel a sense of belonging

Please write in a few significant examples of where you feel / do not feel that you have a sense of 'Belonging' in some key areas in your life.

For example: workplace, family, parish, sport, church, spouse, Britain, pub (See the Notes for Facilitators on the following page for more suggestions)

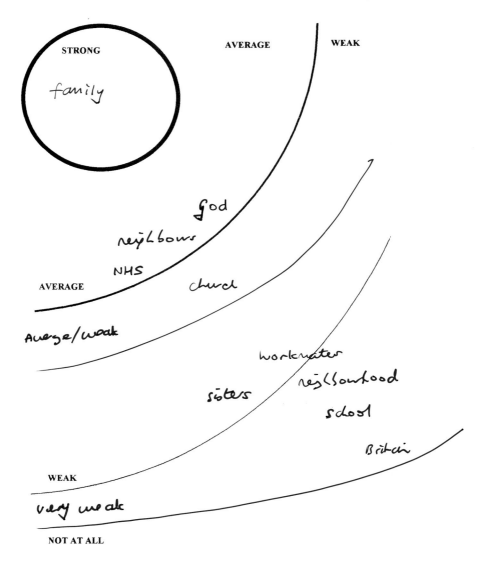

STRONG   **AVERAGE**   **WEAK**

family

god

neighbours

NHS

AVERAGE

church

Auerge/weak

workmates

sisters

neighbourhood

school

Britain

WEAK

very weak

NOT AT ALL

Session One.....Belonging:
Notes for Facilitators

General notes for those preparing and leading study sessions can be found in the Introduction on page 8.

Aims of this session
- to introduce and establish the participant group
- to set the atmosphere for the series of meetings
- to explore the theme of 'Belonging' in a wide sense, in terms of Jesus' message and in terms of possible implications for the participant group

You will need
- either a copy of the Study per participant, or, a photocopy per participant of the prayers, Gospel text and worksheet
- optional: hymnbook, other prayer resources devised by the group
- optional: flipchart or poster, and pens

Welcome
As this is the first session of the series you may need to take some time for people to get to know one another, especially if they are a new grouping. You may choose simply to allow people to chat over a cup of tea or to do an 'icebreaker'.

Sample icebreaker:
Invite people to talk with one other person for one minute each about themselves, their likes and dislikes;

with a second person about their friends and family
with a third about their work and play
with a fourth about their church / club / general support group connections

then, in the full group, invite all those who talked with Person A to tell the rest of the group about them; then Person B....etc.

Note: this may add 20–30 minutes to the session time and may require some adjustments to timing.

Introduction to the theme
Facilitator to read the introductory paragraph.

Suggestions for Opening Worship
- The Prayer of Gathering,
- free prayer

- silence
- prayer devised and led by a member of the group.

Possible hymns from 'Common Ground': *'Dignity and Grace'* (29), *'Gather Us In'* (38) or *'Jesus Calls Us Here To Meet Him'* (66).

Note: All read sections marked 'All'. Individuals read the 'Solo' lines. Read the text around the group. Pause for quiet reflection. You may wish to invite people to share briefly in threes, on what struck them from the prayer. You might then invite a few people to share with the full group.

Exploring our sense and experience of belonging

1) Worksheet: Identifying and reflecting on our own experience of belonging

The purpose of this section is to root the group's reflections in the real lived experience of the participants.

The following list of possibilities is meant as a stimulus, not as an exhaustive check list.

Britain	neighbourhood
brothers / sisters	neighbours
children	parish
church	parishioners
city / rural area	partner
club	political parties
colleagues	politics
community centre	professional associations
denomination	pub
doctor's surgery	race
Europe	religious community
family	retirement complex
football	shops
friends	sport
God	spouse
grandchildren	street
internet	trade union
nationality	workmates

Suggested timing: Introduction: 1–2 minutes; personal reflection and writing time: 3–4 minutes; sharing in threes: 4–5 minutes; invite a few people to provide a flavour of what was said in the threes: 4–5 minutes.

2) Reflecting on our common human experience

Do this in the full group.

Some groups may find a flipchart useful for this part of the session.

Exploring belonging through a passage of scripture

The passage was chosen to allow reflection on how people might 'belong' in relation to Jesus and the Gospel message.

It may help to ask different people to read different paragraphs of the text.

Question 1:   cover this first in groups of three (5–7 minutes) and then seek feedback into the full group (5–8 minutes).

Question 2:   cover this in the full group.

Allow participants to interpret the phrase 'the Christian community' according to their own understanding / experience. Try not to get side-tracked into definitions.

Some groups may find a flipchart useful for the feedback from Question 1 and full group discussion of Question 2.

Invite discussion on why the sense of belonging is perceived as strong/ moderate/ weak or non-existent in the various responses.

You may think about asking a further question about where our contemporary human perceptions might differ from God's perception.

Moving Forward in faith

The group's response may take the form of some concrete action, prayer commitment, research or the like. But, do not force the issue. This is only week one of the series. There will be other time for this kind of question when the group is more established.

Some groups may find a flipchart useful for this part of the session.

Closing Worship

Suggested Prayer: *'Special People'*

Possible hymns from 'Common Ground':
'God to Enfold You' (42), *'Lord of Life'* (76) or
'Through the Love of God our Saviour' (131).

Session Two: Where the heart is.....

...Identity

Welcome and looking back [5 minutes]

Take a few minutes to remember what happened at the last meeting when you considered *Belonging*.

Introduction and Opening Worship [5–10 minutes]

Our theme today is Identity. We are approaching the theme from two angles:

1. *Who we are, what our identity is, how we define ourselves; and*
2. *Who Jesus Christ is, who he is to us, and who we are to him.*

We will look at the first approach through the eyes of the film character, Billy Elliot. It doesn't matter if you've seen the film or not – we'll hear a brief summary of the relevant parts. We will look at the second approach by hearing and praying a passage from Matthew's gospel, where Jesus asks Simon, 'Who do people say I am?'

Reflecting on who we are, and who Jesus Christ is, helps us to greet

*our risen Lord. He will say our name, and we will answer 'Rabboni',
rejoicing in the amazing news that he is alive.*

During your opening worship you may wish to include music, and
to use the following gathering prayer:

> **We gather in this place**
> **To find the still centre within ourselves,**
> **To find peace.**
>
> **We leave behind**
> **The noise and stress of the day**
> **In this time of calm.**
>
> **We open our minds and hearts**
> **that this time**
> **will be fruitful.**
>
> **Here is silence**
> **Here is harmony**
> **Here is hope**
> **Here is God.**

Reading God's Word [5 minutes]

Read the following Psalm Dialogue, based on Psalm 139

Reader:	*O Lord, you search me and you know me*
All:	*You made me, you know me, you love me*
Reader:	*All my ways lie open to you.*
All:	*You, Lord, know the ways of my heart*
Reader:	*For it was you who created my being, knit me together in my mother's womb*
All:	*From the beginning, Lord, you knew me*
Reader	*Thank you for the wonder of my being,*
All:	*I thank you for who I am*
Reader:	*Search us, O God, and know our heart*
All:	*That we might rejoice in your presence*
Pause	
Reader:	*Let us now listen to God's holy word.*

Read the following passage of Scripture:
Matthew 16:13-18 (RSV)

When Jesus came into the district of Caesarea Philippi, he asked his disciples, "Who do people say that the Son of Man is?" And they said, "Some say John the Baptist, but others Elijah, and still others Jeremiah or one of the prophets."

He said to them, "But who do you say that I am?"

Simon Peter answered, "You are the Messiah, the Son of the living God." And Jesus answered him, "Blessed are you, Simon son of Jonah! For flesh and blood has not revealed this to you, but my Father in heaven.

And I tell you, you are Peter, and on this rock I will build my church, and the gates of Hades will not prevail against it."

23

Pause for silent reflection

Prayer

> *You have created us, O God, and you call each of us by name.*
> *You gather us together, so that we may celebrate your care.*
> *Guide us in all we think, do and say*
> *That we may give you glory and praise.*
> *Through Christ, our Lord, Amen.*

Exploring [15 minutes]

Do the following fun quiz, as individuals, either listening to the facilitator reading out the questions and possible answers, or working by yourself.

The questions raise a number of issues about how we define our identity – and how others define our identity for us. **There are no right or wrong answers**. Just mark the answer closest to what you think – the first answer that appeals to you.

Fun Quiz – Who are you?

1. **When you think about your first name,**
   a   You wish you had been given another name
   b   You're happy with the name you have
   c   You just don't think about it at all

2. **If you could have chosen the family you were born into, would you**
   a   Choose a different family
   b   Keep the one you have
   c   Keep your present family, with a few modifications

3. **How well do you think you know yourself?**
   a   Just about average
   b   Very well
   c   Not very well

4. **Is your nationality an important part of your identity?**
   a   Yes, very
   b   Not really
   c   Not sure

5. **If you had to come back for another life, would you**
   a   Choose to be a famous person
   b   Choose to be someone unknown
   c   Come back as yourself!

6. **You make new discoveries about yourself**
   a   Never
   b   Occasionally
   c   All the time

7. **Is your faith an important part of your identity?**
   a   No
   b   Yes
   c   Somewhere in between

8. **When you buy clothes, do you**
   a   Always follow fashion
   b   Sometimes follow fashion
   c   Follow your own tastes

9. When sitting at table for a meal, do you
    a Like to sit at the head of the table
    b Not mind where you sit
    c Where you sit is the head of the table!

10. Is your country
    a Better than other countries
    b Worse than other countries
    c The same as any other country

11. Do you think individuality matters
    a A lot
    b Very little
    c Sometimes

12. You're invited to join a group. Do you
    a Resist — you don't like groups
    b Join readily — you like to feel you belong
    c Give it lots of thought — some groups are OK

13. If people identified you by one of the following, which would it be
    a Your achievements
    b Your looks
    c Your personality

14. Could you imagine changing your identity completely?
    a Easily
    b Not at all
    c Perhaps in some respects

15. The person you most admire is
    a Someone you know personally
    b A well-known public figure
    c Yourself!

There is no scoring in this quiz.
Compare your answers to those of other members of the group.
Do you learn anything new about them?
Do you learn anything new about yourself?
Do you think your identity, who you are, matters to Jesus Christ?
You can discuss any questions that arise from the quiz, or move on to the next section.

Billy Elliot — a study in identity

Billy Elliot is a feel-good film, set in the North East of England against the bleak backdrop of the Miners' Strike in the early 1980's. Billy's mum is dead, and both his dad and brother are out on strike. Times are hard.

Billy attends a weekly boxing class along with many of his friends, but after glimpsing girls practising ballet, he becomes fascinated by the world of dance. Different characters in the film understand their own identity in different ways; how they respond when their self-understanding is challenged is a major theme of the story.

Billy's dad is still mourning his late wife, and is uncertain of his role in the family now she has gone. Billy's brother Tony defines himself over and against 'scabs', those men who cross the picket line to work. Gran is suffering from Alzheimer's: sometimes she is lucid, sometimes confused. Billy's friend Michael is gay, and Billy is the only person he can confide in. Billy's ballet teacher, Mrs Wilkinson, is someone who appears trapped in the locality, with experience of the wider world.

Life in the village is working-class, violent and very macho; against this background, Billy wants to learn ballet – something perceived as feminine, upper-class and entirely useless. Billy negotiates this identity minefield helped by a letter his mother wrote to him when she knew she was dying, and in which she urges Billy to 'always be yourself'.

* * * * * *

Questions raised by the film are useful in reflecting on identity: who we are, as individuals, families and as communities.

- **If our work was taken away from us, how would we feel?**
  Are we, or would we like to be, the breadwinner in the family?
  How important is achievement at work to our identity?
  If we are unemployed, does it affect how we think of ourselves?
  Does God's love for us depend on how hard we work? Why/why not?

- **What do our deepest desires tell us about who we are?**
  What do we dream of for ourselves?
  What would we most wish for in the world?
  Are we achieving our potential?
  Do our deepest desires tell us anything about out Christian faith?

Scripture Study and Discussion [30 minutes]

Identity and Jesus Christ

Read again the gospel passage from Matthew, out loud or individually.

Discuss the following:

1. How does Jesus describe himself here? In what other ways does he describe himself?
2. What is the significance of other people's perception of who Jesus is?
3. Why does Jesus expect a different answer from the disciples?
4. What are the consequences of describing Jesus as Simon Peter does?
5. Jesus changes Simon's name. Why? How is this significant?
6. How do we define ourselves as disciples of Christ? Is this an important aspect of who we are?
7. Is my Christian identity more to do with my individual relationship with Christ, or my belonging to a Christian fellowship / church?

Individual Reflection

led by Facilitator

Reflective music is played (see suggestions in notes). The facilitator reads the following, slowly and meditatively, pausing as suggested:

> *Let us imagine we are sitting amongst the disciples in Caesarea Philippi. Jesus is present. The atmosphere is informal and relaxed.* ***(Pause 30 seconds)***

> *Jesus asks us what other people are saying about him, about who he is and what significance he has. We answer from our own, contemporary experience.* ***(Pause 30 seconds)***

> *Then he asks us who we say he is. Again, we answer him from our heart, saying who he is to us, and what he means.* ***(Pause 30 seconds)***

> *He addresses us, giving us a new name. What would each of us like that name to be? What gift would we most like from the Lord? We ponder in silence.* ***(2 minutes silence)***

The Facilitator may invite the group to share any insights they have received.

The Reflection leads into the Closing Worship.

Closing Worship

[5 minutes]

Facilitator: **Let us give thanks to the God who made us, gives us life and saves us.**

Response to each verse:
> *"I thank you for the wonder of my being"*

You made me, O Lord
and you know me.

You give me life, O Lord
and nurture me with your word.

You help me discover who I am, O Lord
and you reveal yourself to me.

You challenge me to proclaim your reign, O Lord,
and you call me to glory.

Prayer (together):

Loving God, you have given us Jesus Christ
our Redeemer and our friend.
In him, we see your love made visible.
By the power of his Spirit,
Let us strive for justice, unity and peace.
By his grace, bring us to glory
When we will see you face to face
And be transformed,
The wonder of our being
Perfected in your presence.
Bless us, now and always
Through Jesus Christ our Lord.   Amen.

Moving Forward in Faith
[5 minutes]

Take a few moments to consider what you have gained from today's study session, and what you will take away with you. Next week we consider *Culture*. To prepare, you might like to read 1 Corinthians 1: 18-25. Think about what makes up our culture in Britain today. Think about what Paul writes about a culture based on Christ. Ask yourself how at home you feel in contemporary culture, and in Christian culture. Don't worry about how far you get in your reflections – that's what the next session is for.

Session Two.....Identity:
Notes for Facilitators

General notes for those preparing and leading study sessions can be found in the Introduction on page 8.

Aims for the session

To explore the theme of identity—who we are, who Jesus is to us and who we are to him.

The ministry of Jesus was personal. He listened to people, spoke to them, touched them, healed them, forgave them—and *called them by name*. Understanding our own identity, as individuals and as the community of disciples, is understanding who it is Christ ministers to. And just as our understanding of our own identity is important, so is our understanding of the identity of Jesus Christ. Jesus Christ calls us friends, and so we are. We acknowledge him as our risen Lord, and so he is. Who we are is important to him; and who he is, is vital to us.

Points to note about the theme

- Identity is not static, but rather dynamic.
- In relationship, we discover identity. A baby grows in awareness of who she/he is, identifying the other as 'ma ma' and 'da da'. So we first define ourselves in terms of who we belong to.
- We are taught our identity: what is our name; which family we belong to, our place in that family – who we resemble etc.
- We gradually discover and assert our individual identity – likes and dislikes, friends, and eventually belief-systems.
- We define our individual and family identity over and against other individuals and families; our community over and against others; our country too.
- Expectations and societal norms lead us to conform or to stand out.
- Experience sees us grow in self-understanding and self-definition, deliberately putting ourselves in relationship with others (and with God) to develop who we are.

Jesus identifies himself:

In relation to the Father,	In terms of his Mission/destiny,
In terms of history,	In terms of his gifts or powers,
In terms of family,	In terms of disciples/friends.

Worship

Suggested songs for Opening Worship: *Be Still and know that I am God* Mission Praise (48), *Meekness and Majesty* – Common Ground (86)

For Closing Worship: *Spirit of the Living God* – Common Ground (116), *Jesus, you are changing me* – Mission Praise (389)

Exploring—Fun Quiz
This is intended to be light-hearted, an introduction to help get the discussion going and not threatening in any way. There is no need to dwell too deeply on the questions or answers – though of course the quiz may prompt good, relevant conversation on identity that is worth pursuing. You may like to consider beforehand ways in which individuals could share the outcomes, or people may prefer to keep their results private.

Scripture study: Identity and Jesus Christ
This is the heart of the meeting; the time given to it should reflect this.

Individual Reflection
The purpose of this is essentially to encourage those present to listen to the voice of the Lord.

Suggested music (all available on 'Relax More' from Classic FM):

Spiegel im Spiegel – Arvo Pärt; Theme from Schindlers List
Handel – Largo; Barber – Adagio for strings

Additional Resources
Video of the film Billy Elliot – appropriate scene illustrating theme (e.g. confrontation between Billy and his dad, when his dad removes him from the ballet class)

Further questions for discussion:
If you have extra time, or want to miss out one of the sections of the chapter, you may wish to use these additional questions:

(1) How much is our identity defined by gender?

Are we pushed into roles by cultural convention?
Do we categorise people according to stereotypes?
What are our attitudes to people who break with convention?

(2) Do we have identifiable 'enemies', over and against whom we define ourselves?

Do we find ourselves in 'us and them' situations?
With whom do we most firmly disagree?
Who, or what, do we see as the greatest
threat to our identity?

(3) If our memory begins to fail, do we begin to lose our identity?

What is it that makes us who we are?
How important is memory in our
understanding of identity?
Does nostalgia for the past shape who
we are?

Session Three: Where the heart is.....

...Culture

Welcome and looking back   [10 minutes]

Take a few minutes to remember what happened at the last meeting of the group, when you considered *Identity*.

Opening Worship   [5 minutes]

Open in worship, during which you may wish to use the following prayer:

> *Leader:*   **Loving God**
> **Open our hearts**
>
> *All:*   **So that we may feel the breath and**
> **play of your Spirit.**
>
> *Leader:*   **Unclench our hands**
>
> *All:*   **So that we may reach out to one**
> **another,**
> **And touch and be healed.**

Leader:	***Open our lips***
All:	***That we may drink in the delight and wonder of life.***
Leader:	***Unclog our ears***
All:	***To hear your agony in our humanity.***
Leader:	***Open our eyes***
All:	***So that we may see Christ in friend and stranger.*** ***Breathe your spirit into us*** ***And touch our lives with the life of Christ.*** ***Amen***

Anon. New Zealand

You may now wish to include a worship song, or move into the Scripture reading.

Reading God's Word [5 minutes]

Read the following passage from Scripture:
1 Corinthians 1: 18–25 (Good News)

> ***Voice 1:*** *For the message about Christ's death on the cross is nonsense to those who are being lost; but for us who are being saved it is God's power.*

> ***Voice 2:*** *The scripture says: "I will destroy the wisdom of the wise and set aside the understanding of the scholars". So then, where does that leave the really wise? Or the scholars? Or the skilful debaters of this world? God has shown that this world's wisdom is foolishness. For the world in all its wisdom made it impossible for people to know him by means of their own wisdom. Instead by means of the so-called "foolish" message we preach, God decided to save those who believe.*

Voice 3:   *Jews want miracles for proof, and Greeks look for wisdom. As for us we proclaim the crucified Christ, a message that is offensive to the Jews and nonsense to the Gentiles; but for those whom God has called both Jews and Gentiles, this message is Christ who is the power of God and the wisdom of God.*

Voice 1:   *For what seems to be God's foolishness is wiser than human wisdom, and what seems to be God's weakness is stronger than human strength.*

Exploring   [20 minutes]

Paul recognised the different cultures he was dealing with and made a clear bid for a culture based on Christ.

Culture is one of those words which we use without thinking and assume that we all mean the same thing by it. It is worth taking a few minutes to hear from each other what it means for us.

1.   Either (A):

With your neighbour, talk about what culture means to you.

Feedback onto the flipchart. Does anything surprise you? Anything you feel it is important to hold on to? Are there things in our culture which would be hidden to an outsider?

Or (B):

It is particularly difficult to identify characteristics of our own culture. In groups of four or five, look at the statements about our Western culture (over the page). Lay out the photocopied strips of paper on the table and read them together. Decide together which you agree with most, and which you disagree with most. Use the blank sheets of paper to add your own ideas.

Feedback to the group on your first choices, and reason for the choice.

2. How do we know that we belong to this culture we are talking about? What might be a list of criteria?

money makes the decisions in our society

we admire youth and have little respect for old age

appearance is everything; we are obsessed with the body beautiful

our lifestyle assumes that the environment will just keep on giving

our attitudes are manipulated by the media

we live in a blame culture

we live by the adage " as long as it feels all right"

Scripture discussion questions
[20 minutes]

Whether you chose to do exercise (A) or (B), spend some time reflecting on our culture in relation to the reading from 1 Corinthians.

3. What would be considered "wise" within our society yet is challenged by the foolishness of the Gospel?
4. What are the things we "worship" perhaps more than the "crucified Christ"?
5. Why do you think that is?

Listening
[15 minutes]

Sometimes hearing a story from another culture can help us to be more aware of our own. Either allow time for people to read the story opposite, or invite some members of the group to read the story of Elimé Gonzales.

This is a story which tells us something about belonging and something about the Dominican Republic's culture.

6. Does it have echoes in our own society?
7. Does it add anything to your list of criteria identified for knowing that you belong? (see number 2.)

Elimé Gonzales stands facing the four soldiers of the Dominican Republic. 'I am not going to leave' she shouts. They don't say anything but look round nervously at the group of people who, armed with notebooks and pens, start to scribble down what is happening.

Photo: Christian Aid/
Christina Parsons

Elimé continues 'I will not leave. I go to school here. I belong here and it is my right to be here. You go! Leave us alone!' The outburst from the 12 year old girl and the presence of the witnesses perturbs the soldiers. They change their mind about deporting Elimé and her family. 'Let's just leave them', they mutter, and walk off. Elimé tells me they have never been back.

Elimé is a Dominico-Haitian whose parents crossed the border from neighbouring Haiti in search of a better life. Like thousands of other Haitians and Dominico-Haitians there, Elimé and her family feel a sense of belonging in the Dominican Republic. Elimé, because she was born there and her family, because they have spent so long living there.

The government wants them for cheap labour but is not willing to give legal documentation and often threatens deportation. Without documents, they can't access schools or health services. They often use them as a scapegoat for all their problems "those illegal immigrants!" (whether they have legal status or not)

Many Dominicans work happily alongside the Dominico-Haitians but there are those who are very racist—they accuse the Haitians of trying to invade the country and bringing AIDS, malaria and suspect religious practices with them

The objective of the soldiers who came to Elimé's house was deportation of her and her family. Like many who endure deportation, Elimé has documentation proving that she is a Dominican citizen. 'That doesn't matter', she says. 'They just take your document and rip it up. If you offer them money, they will take it and let you go, but then take someone else of the same colour in your place'.

From Christian Aid; Latin American and Caribbean team

Moving Forward in Faith [15 minutes]

Just as stories from other cultures can challenge or affirm our own, so too should the "culture of Christ".

8. What would be some illustrations that we find our identity in Christ?

9. Are there overlaps between the values of our culture and the values of the Kingdom?

10. Are there areas where these values are in conflict?

During the next week, try to be aware of when these cultures overlap and come into contact. Keep a note of this in your own life and in the life of your community. Watch the news and the TV with particular attention.

Closing Worship. [5–10 minutes]

In preparation for worship, take a footprint and as you sit quietly, think of one step you might take towards a Kingdom culture. You may wish to write this on the footprint.

During your closing worship you may wish to sing a worship song, before reading Kate Compston's prayer.

During the reading of the poem let us lay our feet towards the cross as a sign of our renewed commitment to the gospel and to our culture, where it brings life for all.

Leader:

> *Oh God*
> *Who am I now?*
> *Once, I was secure*
>> *In familiar territory*
>> *In my sense of belonging*
> *Unquestioning of*
> *The norms of my culture*
>> *The assumptions built into my language*
>> *The values shared by my society.*
> *But now you have called me out and away from home*
> *And I do not know where you are leading.*
>
> *I am empty, unsure, uncomfortable.*
> *I have only a beckoning star to follow.*

Allow some time in silence or with a familiar chorus or taped music for people to place their feet on the path to the cross. Then say together:

All:

Journeying God
Pitch your tent with mine
So that I may not become deterred
By hardship, strangeness, doubt.
Show me the movement I must make
    Toward a wealth not dependent on possessions
    Toward a wisdom not based on books
Toward a strength not bolstered by might
Toward a God not confined to heaven
But scandalously earthed, poor, unrecognised.
Help me to find myself as I walk in others' shoes.

Kate Compston

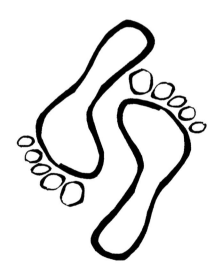

Session Three.....Culture:
Notes for Facilitators

General notes for those preparing and leading study sessions can be found in the Introduction on page 8.

Aims of this session:

To identify the hallmarks of our own society's culture and to explore how we know that we belong to it.
To affirm and to challenge what we accept in our own culture in the light of our understanding of Jesus life and a "kingdom culture".

You will need:

- Volunteers to lead worship and read the story
- Strips of paper with the statements for exercise B, photocopied from page 36 plus strips of paper for participants to add their own thoughts and, if you wish, postcards
- Cut outs of feet for final worship (you could photocopy and enlarge the feet on page 39)
- Free-standing cross for the closing worship, which you could place in the centre of the group

Notes on the theme

In many ways, culture may be a difficult subject to discuss, especially if all the participants come from the same culture.
It is important to remember that a definition of culture today is not only the artistic achievements of any community or indeed the peculiar individual habits and customs, but includes the different ways a community responds to the basic human needs of its members – physical, social and emotional.

Evidence of culture will reflect the underlying values of that community and can be foundational in our sense of identity.

Because we are challenging something which is fundamental to our everyday life, it is even more important to take this session very slowly. Delay on questions 1 and 2 (Exploring) if that seems important and don't worry about trying to finish all the questions.

Opening Worship

Suggested songs: *If you believe and I believe* (Zimbabwe) – Common Ground (62); *O Lord hear my prayer* (Taize) – Songs of God's People (85)

Exploring

In deciding whether to use exercise A or B it may be helpful to know whether your group talks easily together. Exercise B is an easier way for strangers or people who find it hard to speak in a large group to contribute.

Exercise A. It is important to emphasise that there are no right and wrong answers here. Ensure that everyone's answers are noted and take the opportunity to check out what people mean if it is unclear. Using a poster/flipchart, write the word CULTURE in the middle and add the answers as given. You may wish to divide answers into what is seen and what is unseen; i.e. if a stranger were to come to our community, what evidence would there be for the culture and what underlying values might it be harder to detect.

Exercise B. This exercise is known as ranking and allows people to talk in small groups. As the group work together to agree on the placing of the statements in order, they are also making their own arguments for and against. Ensure that there are blank pieces of paper for people to add their own ideas.

The statement the group agrees with most is at the top, the one they disagree with most is at the bottom, and the others are placed in between. Each card will need to be discussed separately, if the final decision is to be a considered one. Encourage people to consider if the statements have equal value.

You could add some postcards of popular culture if you think it would be helpful (e.g. a piper in the glen, bottles of whisky, croft).

As the facilitator feeds back from the discussion, try to discern the values which underlie the cultural norms.

Listening: The story of Elimé

This comes from Christian Aid's partner Onè Respé. Onè Respé unites Dominicans, Dominico-Haitians and Haitians to reflect on and stand up against the forces and systems that exclude them from society. The activities of the group include health care, popular bible reading and psychological therapy. Children also have access to small schools and summer camps and take their message about racism to schools in the area through drama and dance.

It also ran an emergency support programme in response to the massive increase in deportations last year when some 15,000–20,000 people were deported to Haiti. This mass of deportations was a backlash against the report issued by the Organisation of American States criticising the Dominican Government's treatment of Haitian migrant workers and the denial of citizenship to children born to Haitians in the Dominican Republic. The Onè Respé emergency programme included workshops on human and migrants' rights, legal aid and training of teams of witnesses like those who supported Elimé.

This is a strong story and there might be a tendency to focus on the ills of the Dominican Republic rather than on what we can learn about our own. You may need to prompt conversation towards our own treatment of asylum seekers and refugees.

Closing Worship
Suggested song: *Here I am Lord –* Common Ground (50)

Session Four: Where the heart is.....

...Home

Welcome and looking back [5 minutes]

Take a few minutes to recap on your reflections since the last meeting of the group, when you considered *Culture*.

Introduction and Opening Worship [10 minutes]

Open in worship, during which you may wish to use the following prayer:

> *Generous God*
> *Thank you for my home and for all places of hospitality.*
> *Thank you for food to give me strength and furniture to rest my body.*
> *Thank you for photographs to hold my memories.*
> *Thank you for the door to open to friend and stranger,*
> *And for the door to shut when I need my peace.*

Compassionate God
Help me hold in my heart those who cannot say this prayer -
Those who depend on hospitality and cannot offer it
Those who find no hospitality
Those whose house is no home.

Loving God
We remember that wherever we live, our true home is in you.
Amen

Read the following verses from Psalm 107, verse 1–9 (Revised English Bible)

It is good to give thanks to the Lord, for his love endures for ever. So let them say who were redeemed by the Lord, redeemed by him from the power of the enemy and gathered out of the lands, from east and west, from north and south. Some lost their way in desert waste lands: they found no path to a city to live in.

They were hungry and thirsty, and their spirit was faint within them.

So they called to the Lord in their trouble, and he rescued them from their distress:

He led them by a straight and easy path until they came to a city where they might live.

Let them give thanks to the Lord for his love and for the marvellous things he has done for mankind: he has satisfied the thirsty and filled the hungry with good things.

You may now like to include music in your worship, or proceed with the rest of the session.

Reading God's Word [5 minutes]

Read the following passage from Scripture:
Luke 15: 11–32 (Revised English Bible)

There was once a man who had two sons; and the younger son said to his father, "Father, give me my share of the property." So he divided his estate between them.

A few days later the younger son turned the whole of his share into cash and left home for a distant country, where he squandered it in dissolute living. He had spent it all, when a severe famine fell upon that country and he began to be in need. So he went and attached himself to one of the local landowners, who sent him on to his farm to mind the pigs. He would have been glad to fill his belly with the pods that the pigs were eating, but no one gave him anything.

Then he came to his senses: "How many of my father's hired servants have more food than they can eat," he said, "and here am I, starving to death! I will go at once to my father, and say to him, 'Father, I have sinned against God and against you; I am no longer fit to be called your son; treat me as one of your hired servants.'" So he set out for his father's house.

But while he was still a long way off his father saw him, and his heart went out to him; he ran to meet him, flung his arms round him, and kissed him. The son said, "Father, I have sinned against God and against you; I am no longer fit to be called your son." But the father said to his servants, "Quick! Fetch a robe, the best we have, and put it on him; put a ring on his finger and sandals on his feet. Bring the fatted calf and kill it, and let us celebrate with a feast. For this son of mine was dead and has come back to life: he was lost and is found." And the festivities began.

Now the elder son had been out on the farm; and on his way back, as he approached the house, he heard music and dancing. He called one of the servants and asked what it meant. The servant told him, "Your brother has come home, and your father has killed the fatted calf because he has him back safe and sound." But he was angry and refused to go in.

45

His father came out and pleaded with him; but he retorted, "You know how I have slaved for you all these years; I never once disobeyed your orders; yet you never gave me so much as a kid, to celebrate with my friends. But now that this son of yours turns up, after running through your money with his women, you kill the fatted calf for him." "My boy," said the father, "you are always with me, and everything I have is yours. How could we fail to celebrate this happy day? Your brother here was dead and has come back to life; he was lost and has been found."

Discussion [45–50 minutes]

Home is not just the house we live in, but our wider environment.

"When we talk of going home, we don't mean the house, we mean the island."
Harris resident on Radio Scotland, May 2002

"We're Glaswegians."
Glasgow schoolchildren, who had written a song for the European Union, in response to being asked whether they were Scots, British, or Europeans.

(*The Herald*, 10 May 2002)

(1) What would your perfect home offer?

Discuss what you look for in a home; and what 'home' means.

Does our Christian faith affect our attitude to our homes?

Is one's address one's home?

Think of an 8-year old's way of writing their address:

> Alex McLeod
> 3 Anywhere Gardens
> Tannochbrae
> near Glasgow
> Scotland
> Britain
> Europe
> the Western Hemisphere
> the World
> The Solar System
> the Milky Way
> the Universe

Which if these is Alex McLeod's home?

46

We live in a world of imperfection, and for most of us, things fall short of the ideal, but we can imagine what our perfect home might include. The Bible is full of stories about homes: the perfect home that was the Garden of Eden; Noah's preservation of a home for life after the flood; the exile of the People of Israel; the failures of God's people to build a just home afterwards. These passages speak of God as creator, Father, and, above all, provider—the one who cares about our comfort and security and provides for our physical and emotional needs. The New Testament has more to say on the subject. Jesus was homeless at birth, having 'no place to lay his head', though 'foxes have holes and birds have their nests'. His vision of home lay in his relationship with the Father, and he promised his disciples that he had prepared a place, or an ultimate home for them, in God's house.

(2) What are the threats to a perfect home?
What can we lose from our image of the perfect home, and still have one that is comfortable, acceptable or satisfactory? And if we fell short of that, would we be homeless?

> ### The 'carrier bag game'.
>
> Each person has an ordinary carrier bag.
>
> Imagine you are in a town which has just been invaded by an enemy who has given you 5 minutes to leave your house.
>
> What would you put in the bag to take over the border to safety?

Homes are one of the key features of social distinction. People live in a 'good' area of town, or 'on the wrong side of the tracks'. Finance and insurance companies make blanket decisions based on postcodes about whether or not to offer services, or about how much they cost. Some employers won't take people on if they come from certain areas. On the other hand, having a good address gets you places, and puts you in a position to make contacts and get jobs.

47

Think about the story of the prodigal son, particularly the difference between the father's and the older brother's reactions to the return of the young man. Of course, he had been wasteful, he had brought on his own downfall, but the father welcomed him nonetheless. Yet we feel sympathy with the older brother – everything he says is true. But if we follow his line, there is no way back for his younger brother.

(3)   Some of us have no home, or live in areas we are unhappy with. How does my situation affect my attitudes to others?

Do we as a society today offer people a fresh start when they have gone wrong, or are experiencing hardship?

How do the actions of the father in the Bible passage both challenge and encourage us?

Our home, in its widest sense, says things about us. We have already looked at our personal and group identity in previous sessions, and at the culture in which we live. Let us now consider our homes as an expression of our identities and of our Christian culture.

(4)   What does my home say about me?

What would a stranger visiting for the first time know about me from where I live?   Is my home a place of worship, sharing or meditation? Is God present at times of celebration?—and at times of trial or sadness? Where is my spiritual home?

Read and Reflect   [10–15 minutes]

Read the following passage, and then spend some time in silent personal reflection:

A personal experience of home

For the psalmist, finding a place 'where they might live' was the opportunity for those who were lost to be redeemed. By redeemed, I understand that they were able to live a fulfilled life, and to share actively in their community.

For most of the last 20 years, I have made a decent living out of working with and for people who are homeless. At the same time, I have been able to give my own family a secure base, to participate in their growing up. Over the next few years, I expect to watch them leave, and work their way towards homes of their own.

20 years ago, I lived and worked on a housing estate in Rochdale, Lancashire. My job was to support the residents in activities to make the place a better home—youth club; old people's drop-in centre; community carnival; constant attempts to improve the housing repairs service and the general environment. But I realised that for some, particularly young tenants, getting involved in these things was too much to ask.

The estate was the place in town where nobody wanted to live. If you needed somewhere quickly, there were empty flats, and you could move in pretty well at once. But people with any choice would steer clear—only those who were desperate would move in. Of course, many of those had been homeless. In the early 1980s, they were probably also unemployed, and there were plenty of drugs around on the estate—there was even a TV documentary made about its drug problem. There are still many such schemes throughout the UK today.

Colleagues in social work or probation would work hard to find these homeless people somewhere to live, and they often thought they were finding them a home. But getting a roof over their heads was not the whole answer—they were still lost. They had an address, but no community. In fact they were often despised by the established people on the estate, in the fine British tradition of blaming the victim. Many had no family to support them, and their identity had often been shattered by experiences leading to social work care or other institution.

These were my neighbours.

There was one lad who did start to get involved with the tenants association. He had moved in with nothing, and in the way of things, once he had shown willing, people rallied round. Someone put up an old bed that they were ready to throw out, and we gave him some sheets. He got a single electric ring from somewhere, so at least he could heat up a can for his tea. One day I called round, and got no answer. This carried on for a week or so, and eventually the Housing Office went in, and he was gone. It's called 'abandonment'—when someone moves out without giving notice or handing the keys in. I've never seen him since. I still wonder who abandoned whom. In contrast, for my wife and me, living in this scheme has been one of the happiest times of our life. We had two incomes and no kids—financially, we were the best off people in the place. There were pressures, but we could always get away for the weekend if we needed to. And we had great friendships—a far wider range of ages, races, and backgrounds amongst our neighbours than we now have in douce Portobello.

The 'road to a city where we might live' is not necessarily—and probably not usually—a 'straight and easy path'. Of course you don't have to be homeless to be lost, and people who are homeless are not cut off from God. But a firm base from which to live one's life, to grow spiritually as well as physically, is something we all need.

****

Suggestions for personal reflection:

- Have I experienced housing areas similar to the one described? Do they have to exist?
- People living side by side can have very different experiences of the same environment. Is the difference made just by material circumstances, which is what the writer identifies?
- Is the psalmist right about "a straight and easy path"?

Moving Forward in Faith [5-10 minutes]

Take a few moments to consider what you have gained from today's study session, how it relates to previous sessions, and what you will take away with you. If you want to find out more about how local people can help with homelessness in your area, the Scottish Churches Housing Agency can help by providing information, speakers and advice on getting involved.

Closing Worship [5-10 minutes]

During your closing worship, you may wish to include music, and to use the following prayer:

O God, the Maker of all things,
give the people of this land what we need to make
homes for all.
Give us the secure foundations of justice,
the rough-hewn rock of determination,
the reliable tools of co-operation and trust
and the delight of human artistry.
Bless our labour,
fire our imagination,
grace us with your own hospitality
that we who find a home in you
may struggle to see a place of welcome and safety
for all.
We make our prayer in the name of the one who
made his home among us,
Jesus Christ our Lord.
Amen

John McLuckie

Session Four.....Home:
Notes for Facilitators

General notes for those preparing and leading study sessions can be found in the Introduction on page 8.

Aims for the Session

This session looks at 'home' in the context of what we already know about belonging, identity and culture. It recognises that home is a significant part of our whole being, and asks participants to consider what being without a meaningful home implies for people's lives. It looks at the parable of the Prodigal Son and what it implies for life today. It considers the spiritual dimension of our homes, and suggests that we are working towards being at home with God in our relationship with Him. The reflection raises a contrast between the author and someone whose experience of home, at a particular time in their life, was an unsettled one. The session presumes that people participating have a home they are reasonably 'at home' with.

You will need:

- Flipchart and marker pens if you are brainstorming
- A supermarket carrier bag for each participant
- A supply of pens and paper for people to write their own thoughts under section 6

Worship

Start by asking (preferably in advance) one of the group to read the prayer, and another the first psalm,
Suggested songs for Opening Worship: *Be still, for the presence of the Lord* – Common Ground (12); *Christ's is the world in which we move* – Songs of God's people (21); *The Servant King* – Common Ground (128)
For Closing Worship: – *Inspired by love and anger* – Common Ground (63); *Soften my heart, Lord* – Mission Praise (606)

Discussion

1 What would your perfect home offer?

This can be done by brainstorming – asking people to call out what occurs to them, and noting it on a sheet of paper. The basic rule is that everybody's suggestion is valid, and should not be criticised. At the end of the exercise, you should pull the suggestions together, and examine them to see if there are things that conflict with one another, and whether they add up to a complete whole, adding or subtracting things from the list accordingly.

Examples of the sort of answer that will come up might be:

Shelter; comfort; privacy; security; self-fulfilment; bringing up a family; love; a place in the community; opportunities for offering hospitality; retreat; identity.

If things are going slowly, you can ask a few questions to encourage discussion, e.g.:

Is there anything that is common to every home in the world, whether it's in Scotland, Greenland, the rain forest or the Sahara?

What do people first do when they move into a new home? e.g., decorate (to create personal identity); throw a party (to offer hospitality, to demonstrate community).

Look at the box with Alex McLeod's address. Which of these is Alex McLeod's home?

2 What are the threats to a perfect home?

Likely responses –

Divorce/separation; loneliness; bad neighbours; can't afford it; war/flood/earthquake or other disaster; eviction; family disputes.

Once people have thought about the things that would prevent a home from being 'perfect', start a discussion about how many of the things listed in question 1 can be removed, and still leave one with a home, even if it's not perfect? There is certainly room for debate on this one – I once had a heated discussion with a group of primary 3 children as to whether it could be a home if it didn't have a TV!

Other topics for discussion would include:

In our culture, most people's home is static – but people move house during their lifetime, and there are nomads and travellers. Can we be at home and on a journey at the same time?

What does it mean to be homeless?

Who becomes homeless? – in the UK; in the world.

3 What is our attitude to people who have no home, or who live in run-down areas?

Use the older brother's attitude in the story of the prodigal son to explore how we provide routes back into the mainstream for people such as drug users, alcoholics and ex-prisoners. From there, think about how we see people who are 'other' – refugees or asylum seekers, or just people who live in a different area or have different values to ourselves.

4 What does my home say about me?

Start with practical, tangible things – the garden, how many people live in the house, how close it is to the neighbouring house, whether there are clues about people's work or their stage in life. You can stop the discussion at that point if people seem unwilling to go deeper, but asking about the photos or pictures on the walls, what books or music are present, what evidence there is of hobbies or enthusiasms, gives the opportunity to look at how a home holds people's personal stories.

A way of encouraging this discussion is the 'carrier bag game'. Give each person an ordinary carrier bag. Tell them they are in a town which has just been invaded by an enemy who has given them 5 minutes to leave their house. What would they put in the bag to take over the border to safety? Give them a carrier bag to make the exercise more 'real' – since they won't have the things on their person, they can write on slips of paper what they are. But don't let them get away with things that wouldn't fit in the bag!

Reflection: A personal experience of home

Ask people to read the passage by themselves and to use the suggested themes for reflection. This reflection should be a personal one, and about 10 minutes of silence seems about right.

Moving Forward in Faith

People often want to know about practical things they can do to help. The Scottish Churches Housing Agency advises local Churches on getting involved in helping people who are homeless in their own area. If you want to find out more, contact the Agency at
28 Albany Street, Edinburgh EH1 3QH, tel 0131 477 4500, e-mail *scotchho@ednet.co.uk* ; or via the website: *www.churches-housing.org*
In England, the Churches National Housing Coalition does similar work: CNHC, Central Buildings, Oldham Street, Manchester M1 1JT, tel 0161 236 9321, e-mail *brendan.bowles@justhousing.org.uk* or via the website: *www.justhousing.org.uk*

These two organisations link in partnership with CHAS (Catholic Housing Aid Society) to organise Homelessness Sunday, the last Sunday in January each year. This is an opportunity to remember the needs of homeless people in worship. For more information, contact either of them, or email: *dan@chasnational.org.uk* or visit: *www.chasnational.org.uk/homsun.htm*

...*Journey*

Welcome and looking back   [5 minutes]

Take a few minutes to reflect on what happened at the last meeting when you considered *Home*.

Introduction and Opening Worship   [5 minutes]

Open in worship, during which you may wish to use the following prayer:

> *Journeying God,*
> *We are your pilgrim people.*
> *Together we gather,*
> *Together we travel,*
> *Together, let us dance this dance of life.*   *Amen.*

You may now like to include singing of worship songs, or proceed with the rest of the session.

Exploring

[10–15 minutes]

Using a large piece of paper with the word "journey" written on in, spend a short time considering other words for journey, the kinds of journey we make in our lives, what we take with us on our journeys, and how we journey with God.

Reflection

[15–20 minutes]

(See Notes for Facilitators, page 64)

Peter:

It's hot. It's dusty. I'm thirsty but still we walk. We've been walking for three years now. And I still don't know this man I follow.

We're approaching Jerusalem. The closer we get, the gloomier he gets. It worries me. He keeps muttering about death and when he's gone.

If it were anyone else I'd say they were just being melodramatic. This is different. He's the Rabbi, the Master. What would we do without him?

The others might fall apart if trouble comes, but I'd stick by him. I would never walk away from him!

"Peter," he says and smiles, "Come on. I'll wash your tired feet when we get there."

As if! I laugh at his little joke and keep walking.

Judas:

It is hot. It is dusty. I am uncertain but still we walk. We have been walking for three years now. Who is this man I follow?

We are approaching Jerusalem. We have travelled together and I have seen miracles. People love him. Hope and expectation shine in their eyes as they gather and talk of him. Crowds follow – they are desperate for him to perform. This is becoming a circus, a freak show. I am uncomfortable and claustrophobic under the weight of all their neediness. Everything seems upside-down. Just when I think he'll follow some kind of sensible path, he does the opposite. Daily, definitions are turned on their heads.

He has made enemies. He is upsetting the wealthy, the powerful—the very ones he should be courting as allies. Idiot!

This journey to Jerusalem is a death march. I love him. I hate him. He drives me mad. He is mad! This must end.

I make my plans, laugh at some joke, and keep walking.

Jesus:

It's hot. It's dusty. I've been walking all my life! And now, near the end-point of this journey, there are so many questions.

We are approaching Jerusalem. There I will ride into the city on the donkey that awaits me. The crowds will cheer in hopeful expectation of … what? An uprising? Upheaval? A restoration to former glory days? The crowds will cheer and completely miss the point of my mission and message.

Even now, I have the power to choose. We could disband. I could go back home and be a carpenter once more. There in the bitterness of broken dreams and shattered expectations, I'd spend the rest of my days gnawed at by failure and regret. Foxes have holes and birds have nests, but I no longer have claim on a place to rest. I can't go back, only onward. Judas doubts and is uncertain. I see him watching me, hoping that I'll fuel his ambition. I am the kiss of death to his dreams.

He will betray me.

Peter blusters and is too certain. When the cheers turn to jeers, he'll fall from that pedestal of certainty. He will deny me.

Betrayal, denial, death await. Father, this is a hard road to travel!

Steady, steady. We're nearly there now. They've gone to fetch the donkey that will lead me to my doom. I shrug off the darkness, laugh, and keep walking.

****

Questions for silent reflection on the above passages.

1. You are hot, dusty and thirsty. You are walking the road with Jesus. What does it feel like to be walking with this group?

2. As you walk, where are you – in the middle of the group, at the back, on the edge, or walking near Jesus up at the front?

3. Wherever you are in the group, now move closer to Jesus – he is beckoning to you. What is he saying to you?

4. What would you like to say to him?

Reading God's Word [5 minutes]

Read the following passage from Scripture:

Mark 11: 1–11 (NRSV)

The triumphal entry into Jerusalem.

When they were approaching Jerusalem, at Bethphage and Bethany, near the Mount of Olives, he sent two of his disciples and said to them. "Go into the village ahead of you, and immediately you enter it, you will find tied there a colt that has never been ridden; untie it and bring it. If anyone says to you 'Why are you doing this?' just say this, 'The Lord needs it and will send it back here immediately.'" They went away and found a colt tied near a door, outside in the street. As they were untying it, some of the bystanders said to them, "What are you doing, untying the colt?". They told them what Jesus had said; and they allowed them to take it. Then they brought the colt to Jesus and threw their cloaks on it; and he sat on it. Many people spread their cloaks on the road, and others spread leafy branches that they had cut in the fields. Then those who went ahead and those who followed were shouting,

> *"Hosanna!*
> *Blessed is the one who comes in the name of the Lord!*
> *Blessed is the coming kingdom of our ancestor David!*
> *Hosanna in the highest heaven!"*

Then he entered Jerusalem and went into the temple; and when he looked around at everything, as it was already late, he went out to Bethany with the twelve.

Group activity and Questions [30 minutes]

On the spiritual journey how do we get to know God? Jesus says "Follow me." To follow implies movement, a journey, an ongoing process. How can we follow if we are standing still?

To follow implies trust and faith in our guide, which in turn implies relationship. Perhaps the key to following centres on building relationships – with God, through Jesus and with one another, through the power of God's Spirit.

> *'The way to God is the way of creating living, loving relationships; breaking down barriers of fear, hatred and prejudice. It means being prepared to be hurt; being prepared to help whoever needs help without making a judgement about their worthiness to be helped. It means being prepared to confront evil gently but firmly, seeking to transform, not to destroy. It means being prepared to love to the nth degree; being prepared to protect the weak; being fervent for justice and truth; being prepared to seek God's way in every situation, seeking strength from God; not speaking or thinking evil of anyone.'*
>
> John Stevenson

Jesus journeyed to Jerusalem. He sensed that it was not going to be an easy journey. After the cheers of his entry into the city, there were to be jeers, torture and death. In the horror of Good Friday, the journey seemed to go so badly wrong.

Throughout the course of these study sessions, we have been journeying with Jesus on the road to Jerusalem. But what does journey mean? What does it cost? How do we make this journey? What lies ahead, and where are we going? What do we do when we get there? What happens to us if it all goes horribly wrong?

1. (As a group) Draw a life-line of Jesus' life, marking significant points on the way.

2. Draw your group life-line – what have been the significant moments during the study of the last several weeks?

3. What happens when your journey seems to go the wrong way?

4. How do we respond when we see other people struggling on the way?

5. (For personal reflection) On the journey line provided, note the significant points on your journey.

My Journey

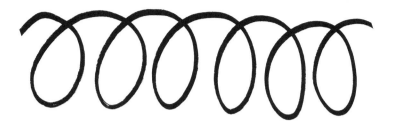

Prayers of intercession [5 minutes]

ONE: *Humble and riding on a donkey,*
ALL: We greet you.

TWO: *Acclaimed by crowds and carolled by children,*
ALL: We cheer you.

THREE: *Moving from the peace of the countryside to the corridors of power,*
ALL: We salute you, Christ our Lord.

ONE: *You are giving the beasts of burden a new dignity;*
TWO: *You are giving majesty a new face;*
THREE: *You are giving those who long for redemption a new song to sing.*
ALL: With them, with heart and voice, we shout 'Hosanna!'

ONE: *Humble and riding on a donkey*
Carrying our expectations,
Defying our definitions,
You ride through the battle-scarred places of your world.

We pray for all areas of tension and conflict,
Where violence and war are normal,
Where life is cheap,
and where the cry of the orphan goes unheard.
We remember those who have no home
but the road on which they walk.

ALL: **Bring healing**
Bring peace
Bring love

ONE: *Humble and riding on a donkey*
Challenging our opinions,
Weeping at our divisions,
You ride among us, your sometimes-bickering children.
We pray for greater love and understanding between the many strands
Of the church, your body here on earth.
Let us hunger for reconciliation between our brothers and sisters.
Let us celebrate our gifts and our diversity!
We remember those who feel excluded and rejected from your body
And who walk their spiritual journey alone.

ALL: **Bring understanding**
Bring patience
Bring love

ONE: *Humble and riding on a donkey*
Bearing our burdens,
Holding our hurts;
You ride with us to the dark, fearful places in our hearts.
We pray for all those who suffer;
For all those who are ill;
For all those who grieve;
We remember those who live in constant fear of exile or eviction
With nowhere safe to lay their head.

ALL: ***Bring heart***
            Bring hope
            Bring love

ONE: *Humble and riding on a donkey,*
ALL: ***We greet you.***

TWO: *Acclaimed by crowds and carolled by children,*
ALL: ***We cheer you.***

THREE: *Moving from the peace of the countryside to the
          corridors of power,*
ALL: ***We salute you, Christ our Lord.***

ONE: *You are giving the beasts of burden a new dignity;*
TWO: *You are giving majesty a new face;*
THREE: *You are giving those who long for redemption a new
          song to sing.*
ALL: ***With them, with heart and voice we shout 'Hosanna!'***

Wild Goose Worship Group (adapted)

Closing Worship   [5–10 minutes]

During your closing worship you may like to include music, and to say together:

> ***"MY LORD GOD, I have no idea where I am going. I do not see the road ahead of me. I cannot know for certain where it will end. Nor do I really know myself, and the fact that I think that I am following your will does not mean that I am actually doing so. But I believe that the desire to please you does in fact please you. And I hope I have that desire in all that I am doing. I hope that I will never do anything apart from that desire. And I know that if I do this you will lead me by the right road though I may know nothing about it. Therefore will I trust you always though I may seem to be lost and in the shadow of death. I will not fear, for you are ever with me, and you will never leave me to face my perils alone."***

Thomas Merton

Session Five .... Journey
Notes for Facilitators

General notes for those preparing and leading study sessions can be found in the Introduction on page 8.

You will need

Prior to the actual session, you will have prepared a central table or a space in the middle of the group. Have a candle and matches in this space. If you're using this study during Lent or Advent, you may like to use a purple cloth, the colour traditionally associated with these times of year. To suggest the theme of journey, gather a small collection of items and place them in the central area by the candle. Items may range from bus tickets, car keys, travel brochures. Wherever your imagination takes you! Overall, you want to create a simple visual aid to help people connect with the theme of 'journey'.

Introduce the theme of this week's session.

As Christians, we are called to follow Jesus. To follow implies movement, a journey, an ongoing process. Through this period of study, we have been journeying with Jesus on the road to Jerusalem. But what does journey mean? What does it cost? How do we make this journey? What lies ahead, and where are we going? What do we do when we get there?

Light a candle, leave a short space for silence…

Opening worship

Before the prayer, explain that the candle is lit to symbolise the journey you will be making together through this study. (It also helps people to gather their thoughts.) It is a useful tool in setting aside a 'sacred space' as you journey together through the session and formally marks the entry into the actual session. After the prayer, the group might like to sing *Come all you People* – Common Ground (18).

Exploring – icebreakers

Before the session, you will need a large piece of paper with the word 'journey' written on it. You will also need a marker pen/s with which to jot down ideas.

Either:—

A buzz group. Have the group think of other words for 'journey' When this is done, ask:

1. Which of these resonates with you the most?
2. Why?
3. What kinds of journeys do we make in our lives and why?
4. What equipment do you need to take on your journey?
5. What equipment do we need to take with us when we journey with God? How do we journey with God?

Or:—

Have the word 'journey' written on sheet, with lots of words for journey—use the dictionary—and then move into the questions. Ask the group –

1. What comes to mind when this word is used?
2. What types of journeys do we make and why?
3. What equipment do you need to take on your journey?
4. What equipment do we need to take with us when we journey with God? How do we journey with God?

Reflection

Before the reflections are read out, invite people to find a comfortable position in which to sit. One way of leading folk into a silent / guided meditation is to get them to concentrate on the rhythm of their breathing. Say something along the lines of – "Breathe in and feel the air flowing into you. Breathe out and feel it flowing from you." Repeat this until you sense people have relaxed.

Have the different sections read by different people. This is useful for a change of pace and voice.

Leave a wee space between each reflection. The readings themselves with spaces should take about 4–5 minutes.

Reflection questions

Flow gently from the reflections into quiet contemplation. The questions have been provided to help people focus.

Quietly, so as not to break the mood, ask the first question. Allow a space for silent contemplation before moving to the next question. Again, silent contemplation. Allow 3–4 minutes for the last two questions. Finish with an 'amen', and take a couple of moments to allow people to gather themselves. Then gently move into the Bible reading.

Reading God's Word

Invite someone from the group to read this meditatively.

Activities and questions

On separate sheets of paper, draw a line, either straight or spiral. Page 1 headed 'Jesus' journey', page 2 headed 'group journey'. This is to be done as a group activity.

In the book, there is a spiral entitled 'My journey'. This is to be done as silent personal preparation to lead into the intercessions. (Depending on time, this can be done as something to take home and reflect on during the course of Holy Week.)

Intercessions.

An opportunity for three people to read. Entire group to read words in bold. You may want to insert a chant each time the group has read the words in bold. *Lord Jesus Christ, Lover of all* (75); '*Jesu Tawa Pano* (65); or *O Lord Hear my Prayer* (94)—all in Common Ground.

Closing Worship.

The facilitator may like to read the closing prayer, and after a silent pause, you may like to sing one or more of the following songs from Common Ground:

Sent by the Lord am I (105); *Jesus Christ is Waiting* (67); *One More Step* (100)

The candle is extinguished.

Acknowledgements

ACTS gratefully acknowledges permission to reproduce copyright material in this publication. Every effort has been made to trace and contact copyright holders.

The Scripture quotations are from:

- The MESSAGE – Copyright (c) by Eugene H. Peterson 1993, 1994, 1995, 1996, 2000, 2001, 2002. Used by permission of NavPress Publishing Group.
- The Revised Standard Version of the Bible, copyright (c) 1946, 1952 and 1971 by the Division of Christian Education of the National Council of the Churches of Christ in the USA. Used by permission. All rights reserved.
- The Good News Bible, used by permission of the Scottish Bible Society.
- The Revised English Bible (c) Oxford University Press and Cambridge University Press 1989.
- The New Revised Standard Version of the Bible, copyright (c) 1989 by the Division of Christian Education of the National Council of Churches of Christ in the USA. Used by permission. All rights reserved.

In addition we acknowledge:

- The extract, in the Introduction, from *The Dark Room* by Rachel Seiffert, published by William Heinemann. Reprinted by permission of The Random House Group Ltd.
- Karl Barth for *Prayer at the start of worship*, from *AFFIRMS* (The Catholic Education Commission - Scotland 1994) adapted for use in Session One, as "A Prayer of Gathering".
- Prayer: *Special People*, used in Session One, author and source unknown.
- The prayer in Session Three beginning "Loving God, open our hearts", anonymous author, from *Out of Darkness: paths to inclusive worship* (Australian Council of Churches 1986).
- Christian Aid for the story and photograph of Elimé Gonzales used in Session Three.
- The prayer in Session Three beginning "Oh God, who am I now?" by Kate Compston. Copyright Kate Compston.
- John McLuckie for the prayer beginning "O God, the maker of all things" in Session Four.

- John Stevenson for the paragraph beginning "The way to God is the way of creative living, loving relationships" used in Session Five.

- The prayer in Session Five beginning "Humble and riding on a donkey" from *Stages of the Way* (Wild Goose Publications 1998) (c) 1998, WGRG, Iona Community, G2 3DH. Adapted by Nikki Macdonald.

- Thomas Merton for the prayer in Session Five beginning "My Lord God, I have no idea where I am going" from *Thoughts in Solitude*. (Burns & Oates, first published in 1958.)

Thanks are due to:

- The study groups in Paisley, Eastwood, Pollockshaws, Broughty Ferry, Inverness, Bathgate, Perth, Wishaw, and Barrhead who piloted the material, and whose comments and suggestions were so helpful.

- The ecumenical team from ACTS who made this project possible:

Alastair Cameron	Tom Moyes
Helen Hood	Linda Rice
Patricia Lockhart	David Sinclair
Nikki Macdonald	Elizabeth Templeton
John McLuckie	Gill Young